YELLOWMAN

BY DAEL ORLANDERSMITH

★

★

DRAMATISTS
PLAY SERVICE
INC.

YELLOWMAN
Copyright © 2002, Dael Orlandersmith

All Rights Reserved

YELLOWMAN was first coproduced by the McCarter Theatre (Emily Mann, Artistic Director), the Wilma Theater (Blanka Zizka and Jiri Zizka, Artistic Directors) and the Long Wharf Theatre (Gordon Edelstein, Artistic Director) in Princeton, New Jersey, on January 10, 2002. It was directed by Blanka Zizka; the set and projection design were by Klara Zieglerova; the lighting design was by Russell H. Champa; the composer was Elliott Sharp; the costume design was by Janus Stefanowicz; and the stage manager was Paul-Douglas Michnewicz. The cast was as follows:

ALMA .... Dael Orlandersmith
EUGENE .... Howard W. Overshown

CHARACTERS

ALMA — Aged 36–43. A large-sized black woman. Her complexion is medium to dark brown-skinned.

EUGENE — Aged 38–45. *Very* fair-skinned, fairly muscular black man.

SETTING

The stage is bare, except for two chairs.

Note: Actors must be able to switch characters to indicate other scenes, places as well as other characters.

YELLOWMAN

PART I

Alma sits in a chair upper stage right on raised platform talking directly to audience except when indicated.

ALMA. There's a fluidity to the heat in South Carolina/ watching certain objects — maybe certain fields of cotton, corn, tobacco/ there seems to be some sort of rippling effect. My mother/ women like my mother and her mother before her talked about the sun — staying in it too long creates illusion/ they — my mother/ women like her and more than likely her mother before her talked in Gullah/ Geechie accents about how *(Voice.)* "da sun can make ya see tings dat ain't dere" or "dat heat is sumpin ya hear." *(Alma.)* Her statements always seemed to end in questions. There were always question marks at the end of her observations as if she wasn't entirely sure of what she felt, heard, saw — moreover they weren't entirely sure as to whether they were entitled to hear, think, or see — truly see. The question marks at the end of their statements were from women who knew their place and the fact that they had opinions about something as simple as sunrays pulled them from their place — the fact that they would question ANYTHING made them "uppity" in the eyes of their peers.

My mother women like my mother and her mother before her toiled/ tugged the soil right beside the men. They were dark therefore not considered pretty/ they were dark and large — therefore sexless. They were sometimes bigger than the men/ their bodies filling space/ in their dresses as they toiled, they looked awkward/ they wore dresses in work — heat for a semblance of femi-

5

ninity/ in heat and toil they craved softness, pliability thinking somehow it would appeal to some man when in fact their sweat dresses made them seem bigger/ more awkward and the fact that they did not carry their bigness with pride — with their large heads and backs in total alignment, they were to be pitied.

They continued to tug/ toil the soil right beside the men — they cursed and prayed in their Gullah/ Geechie voices/ their Ball 'n' Chain voices/ their Gullah/ Geechie / ball 'n' chain voices/ Ma Rainey/ Bessie Smith does the Hucklebuck with Big Mama Thorton and *(Voice.)* "Oh praise God/ help me Lawd git thru another day." *(Alma.)* Always my mother/ her mother before her praised God not for living/ not for happiness/ they did not live/ they were not happy — they existed and they praised Him not totally sure whether or not He existed. They did so because they were taught to/ had to and that there had to be some love somewhere if they prayed long enough/ hard enough. There was no love for them on this plane/ this earthly plane so they praised and prayed in their Gullah/ Geechie/ voices for a space — no matter how meager in heaven. In heaven they would be seen/ loved/ not big/ ugly/ and black in heaven/ in heaven they'd be thin/ light and beautiful. Here on earth the men beat them/ leave them/ they ride them/ they don't make love to them/ they ride them/ the men/ they rode always on top/ men like my father/ they rode/ they entered/ they shot their seed/ then left them.

My mother/ women like my mother and her mother before her took it/ ate it/ accepted it as *(Odelia.)* "one o' dem tings dat mens does do to womens." *(Alma.)* They/ felt they deserved no more/ no more than that/ they felt it was their due for being big, awkward, poor and dark. This is what my mother/ her mother before her believed/ they believed had they been born "rich and high yella," they wouldn't have suffered/ they thanked God that I wasn't born dark/ although too bad I wasn't lighter/ but they thanked God I wasn't dark. My mother and her mother before her believed/ if only they could be light/ light and rich/ if they could marry a light-skinned man, they'd be loved. *(Lights come up on Eugene who sits in a chair downstage left. He talks to the audience unless otherwise indicated.)*

EUGENE. My father was a big, big man and there was something

6

about that bigness — especially if you're a child in the South. I watched my father and men like my father. Black southern men seemed incredibly big — especially men who labored in heat or knew about that heat/ sweat of black men in the South/ the sweat just dripping off their bodies/ their big bodies — particularly darker/ dark men. Man, there was something about that bigness that jet-black bigness/ that down-home bigness/ old time stuff like John Henry or somebody's Robert Johnson song — even though that was way before his time but not really before his time/ John Henry/ Robert Johnson and Hallelujah or moreover in my father's vocabulary — "niggerstuff" — jet-black "niggerstuff." *(Pause.)* He was big, dark, handsome — my father? Oh yeah, my father was handsome. He didn't know it — that he was handsome. Like many dark men who didn't know they were handsome. *(Beat.)*

Sometimes he — my father — would look in the mirror and say "the finest man that ever walked." He'd laugh but really he wouldn't laugh. I'd watch him and the laughter would disappear and he'd turn to — rather on me/ he'd turn on me and I was about nine — maybe ten but I think I was nine and he said *(Robert.)* "Do you think I'm handsome Eugene?" and I said *(Eugene.)* "Yeah, Daddy." Then he stood over me/ towering over me in all his blackness and said with incredible menace *(Robert.)* "Do you think I'd be more handsome if I was high yella like you?" *(Eugene.)* and I gasped you know and inside I'm crying/ screaming and another part of me wants to hurt him, hit him and I balled my fists/ balled them and he looks down at me and there's bourbon in him/ all day he'd been at it/ the bourbon but you'd never know it / that he had bourbon in him unless you knew him well and could smell it. Via this bourbon, all the anger came to and at me. He — my father — "Robert Gaines" as he referred to himself when in his bourbon got mad — real mad and when that happened, the Geechie/ Gullah came out. The standard English that he had so painstakingly studied to rid himself of Russelville/ cutting wood for Georgia Pacific/ that thing in him that would make him feel that he was the darkest and ugliest of all men would come back to him and he in turn would throw it on to me. *(Pause.)* So he looks down on me/ at me. *(Robert.)* "You wanna fight me high yella, huh? You wanna fight? I think your best bet high yella is to get outta my face before I hurt you/ 'cause I will knock your high yella/ red ass down!" *(Pause. Eugene.)* I looked up at Daddy's face/ his dark, dark face/ his mysterious, handsome face and he looked at my light face — my eyes were very open — very wide and within that moment the night before us became very thick between us. My light face looked up at his dark one and he winced — actually winced because as small as I was and as terrified as I was, I also hated him and we both knew within that moment, in a weird way, my hatred was going to rear its head. Somehow we both knew my hatred was stronger than his six foot four frame and within that moment his physical stature meant nothing at all. *(Pause.)* My hate was strong but it always is, isn't it? Hate I mean — pure unadulterated hate.

ALMA. Eugene and I were young once — in the sixties we were young children in the schoolyard. All of us were young in the schoolyard playing. All of us *(Child Alma.)* "Hot peas 'n' butta — come and git yo' suppa!"

EUGENE. *(Child Eugene. Sings.)* "Miss Mary Mack Mack, Mack — all dressed in black black, black — "

BOTH. *(Sing.)* "With silver buttons, buttons, buttons all down her back, back, back."

ALMA. *(Beat.)* I was seven when I first laid eyes on Gene. I saw this little boy — a little older than us — he was nine and in the fourth grade. He looked like he was wearing a suit.

EUGENE. It wasn't a suit.

ALMA. There was the formality of a suit. I went over to him. *(Child Alma.)* "Why you wearin a suit to come to school? All o' us is playin an stuff — you don't never play wit nobody. I see you by ya-self all the time — you wanna play wit us? I know you in the fourth grade but you can be wit us."

EUGENE. It was a button-down shirt. It was my favorite shirt and I felt good wearing it. *(Child Eugene.)* "I'm not wearing a suit. I'm wearing my favorite shirt and that's why and I don't care about me being in the fourth grade and you being in the second grade — I want to play with you." I wanted to say "Let's be friends. I see you all the time in the schoolyard and everybody likes you. EVERYBODY — how do you make everybody like you? How do you make people like you?" That's what I wanted to say but I was a child and I didn't know how.

8

ALMA. I ask him his name and he says —

EUGENE. Eugene Robert Gaines.

ALMA. He says his whole name —

EUGENE. "Eugene Robert Gaines."

ALMA. "You talk funny. Not funny like 'laugh' funny — you does talk nice. You talk like people on TV talk. You don't talk like none o' us. You does talk good — I like it." Then we played —

BOTH. "Hot peas and butter, come and git yo' suppa." We played and yelled and played —

EUGENE. That day I met Alton White. He was friends with Alma first and he just sort of comes up to me. He sees me talking to Alma and just comes up smiling. This small dark boy with dark eyes and a wide, great smile — not malicious in the least. He has a great smile. I look down at him and say "I'm Eugene Robert Gaines. What's your name?" He looks up at me and says *(Alton.)* "My name is Alton — Alton White." *(Eugene.)* We play at lunch and Alton says *(Alton.)* "Eugene let's play after school." *(Eugene.)* I say "What do you want to play?" He grins *(Alton.)* "I wanna play Batman." *(Eugene.)* I say "Okay — does that mean that I play Robin?" He says *(Alton.)* "You wanna play Batman?" *(Eugene.)* I say "yeah," *(Alton.)* "okay."

My heart is beating. My heart never beats like this except when Daddy yells but this is a different kind of heartbeat. This day — the way my heart beats this day is thrilling. There's a raucous, thrilling rhythm in my chest. So we meet after school and Alton comes running out of the school wearing glasses with the arms of his sweater tied around him like a cape and runs straight over to me as Robin. *(Alton.)* "Holy flyin' fish Batman! Gotham City is in trouble!" *(Eugene.)* "Okay Robin — don't panic. I can tell the Joker had something to do with this — probably with the help of Catwoman — "

ALMA. *(Makes Catwoman's gesture and sound.)* "Meow." Alton, Eugene and I are inseparable. I end up playing what they always want to play which is "Batman" or they'd trade "Spiderman" comic books. I hate playing Catwoman. "Why I haveta play her. I wanna play the Joker or the Riddler. I don't wanna play no Catwoman! She ain't cool. I ain't ga play her no more — y'all make me sick!" One day some other kids from Russelville see us playing. One of them says *(Voice 1.)* "Oh you an Alton playin wit dat ole yella boy from St. Stephen. Y'all don play wit us no more — y'all like him 'cause he yella an rich an live in da city limits." *(Eugene stops singing. Alma.)* "I say I play wit who I wanna play wit an y'all need to mind y'all business — Gene is my friend just like Alton my friend!" *(Voice 2.)* "Well if you an Alton ga be friends wit dat yella boy, you can't be friends wit us!" *(Alma.)* "I ain't care! I don't wanna be friends whichy'all anyway."

EUGENE. In the schoolyard, when Alton and I would play, we'd run around the yard and as we ran, we'd extend our arms to the side. It was synchronicity. Both of us running with arms extended. Two boys. Not a light-skinned boy and a dark-skinned boy — TWO BOYS — running. Running despite summer heat. Summer heat can't stop us/ summer heat won't stop us. Once in a while running Alton asked *(Alton.)* "Hey Gene, you think anybody ever ran around the whole wide world?" *(Eugene.)* "No I don't think so." *(Alton.)* "Let's you an me do it Gene. When we git to be older — let's us run around the whole world."

ALMA. There were days when I ran with those guys. I just ran and ran. I didn't know I could run. My mother Odelia — I never called her "Mom" "Mother" or "Mama" — just Odelia — she always made fun of me. *(Odelia.)* "Ole big fat funny lookin' thing can't run — ole fat funny lookin thing can't do nuttin." But I could run. I really began to run. *(Beat.)* One day after school the three of us were playing our "running game." Gene yells —

EUGENE. "Okay, we're going through the jungle. There are vultures on both sides and the sky is filled with crows and you know what that means! That means somebody is gonna die so we gotta run — RUN FAST. We can't let the vultures get us!"

ALMA. — and Alton and Eugene are running real fast and I'm having a hard time catching up. Then Gene turns around and yells —

EUGENE. "You can do it Alma — you run real well — don't let the vultures get you. You can do it — come on Alma."

ALMA. He stops for a second and takes me by the hand. We run together. We run through the jungle. We survive the jungle. We finish running and the three of us fall to the ground –

EUGENE. "I told you! I told you, you could do it! You did it!"

ALMA. We're lying on the grass, Alton, Eugene and I, and I say, "Let's sing the Monkees song!" *(She sings.)* "Hey, hey, we're the

10

Monkees."

TWO BOYS. "People say we're monkeying around/ but we're too busy singing/ to put anybody down."

EUGENE. There was a boy in school named Wyce who was light — if not a little lighter than me. *(Wyce.)* "Why you hanging out with those darkassed Geechies for? Didn't your Momma tell you not to do that?" *(Eugene.)* "No, my Daddy's dark." *(Wyce.)* "Yeah that's right. I forgot. Your momma shouldn't have done that but at least you're light like her."

ALMA. Odelia began to get upset with me not coming straight home from school. *(Odelia.)* "Alma ya got to be mo ladylike. Stop rippin an rarin all over the place. Look at your hair all nappy from sweat. It don't look nice for a girl to be runnin — especially 'cause ya so big. Ya don't look good runnin — ya TOO BIG an Lawd runnin' in dis heat, ya don't wanna git black."

EUGENE. I ask Wyce. "So what I'm light. So what you're light. Who cares? What does it matter?" He looks at me like I'm crazy. *(Wyce.)* "What does it matter? Boy, you wanna look like a spook an talk like some blackass Geechie?"

ALMA. *(Odelia.)* "An when ya grow up, ya should marry a man just like dat Gaines boy, dat purty yella boy. Don't you marry nobody like Alton — darkass like Alton — ole funny lookin nigga — dat boy is BLACK — BLACK and UGLY." *(Alma.)* "Alton ain't ugly — he ain't ugly at all."

EUGENE. I ask Momma, "Momma, how come you're light and Daddy's dark?" *(Thelma.)* "Honey, colored people come in all shades. I just happen to be fairer than your daddy is." *(Eugene.)* "This boy at school — his name is Wyce — he said that you shouldn't have been with Daddy 'cause he's so black." *(Thelma.)* "Eugene — don't pay them any attention. Your father is just as good as anybody else."

ALMA. "How come when I git old and wanna git married, I can't marry somebody who got Alton's color?" *(Odelia.)* "He is too dark, I keep tellin ya — he's too dark — iffin ya dark like that it don't look nice — it look ugly." *(Alma.)* "Yeah, but you dark." *(Odelia.)* "Dat's why I know what I sayin — I dark, fat, Black an ugly — Goan outside an play!"

EUGENE. "Daddy, how come you're dark and live with me and

11

Momma and other light-skinned people here in St. Stephen in the city limits?" *(Thelma.)* "That's 'cause your daddy worked full-time at Georgia Pacific and went to school full-time so we could have a good life." *(Robert.)* "Tell him the truth Thelma. I — Robert Gaines — got out of Russelville because I worked harder than light-skinned people like you and your mother and your grandfather Eugene. But how could YOU know what I mean — YOU'LL never know what I mean."

ALMA. "How come my daddy don live here wit us? Eugene got a momma and a daddy. How come he ain't here? What he look like?" *(Odelia.)* "Yo daddy does be on da road an works hard but one day he gon come back for us an we ga git off dis place an live good. One day Alma we ain't gon slop no hawgs or rake no chicken shit out a yard. Yo daddy ga come back fa us."

EUGENE. Me and Alton trade "Spiderman" comic books. We always trade in school, you know? And one day Alton says *(Alton.)* "Why don't you come to my house Eugene?" *(Eugene.)* And I'm real excited and I said I would you know, but I'm scared in a way because besides certain immediate family, I'd never been to anybody's house before. So we set this time to trade comics and to sketch and draw together because me and Alton are thinking about starting our own comic series. We are going to create our own superhero series.

So on this Saturday, I get all my comics and drawing materials and I go to Alton's house which is close. His house isn't in the city limits but isn't that far from me at all. I get there and Mrs. White — his mother — is on the porch sewing. *(Eugene becomes Mrs. White.)*

EUGENE. "Hello ma'am."

MRS. WHITE. *(Coldly.)* "Hello."

EUGENE. "Are you Alton's mother?"

MRS. WHITE. "Dat's right."

EUGENE. "I'm Eugene Robert Gaines and I'm here to play with Alton."

MRS. WHITE. "Look heah, you say you dat Gaines boy?"

EUGENE. "Yes ma'am."

MRS. WHITE. *(Wary.)* "Robert Gaines yo' daddy?"

EUGENE. "Yes ma'am."

MRS. WHITE. "What you want 'round heah boy?"

EUGENE. "Well like I said Mrs. White, I've come to play with Alton. We were gonna sketch and trade comics — "

MRS. WHITE. "You come 'round heah to laugh at Alton ain't it?"

EUGENE. "No ma'am — I swear! He's my friend — Alton's my friend. I would never — "

MRS. WHITE. "Boy you mus' think I'm stupid ain't it? You think 'cause I ain't got book learnin' that I ain't know why you bring yo' lil red rump 'round heah? You come heah to see how po' we is so you can go back to dat yella momma o' yourn an' pitch black nigga daddy o' yourn an' laugh 'bout how me an my boy does live. Me an my boy is pure blood black/ PURE BLACK — ya hear? You go on 'way from heah! I ain't ga let you laugh at my boy. Let you steal from my boy! Ya momma send you 'round here to thief from him? You an ya momma ain't nuttin but some thieves — Git 'way from heah."

EUGENE. I look up and see Alton staring down at me. He's half hiding behind the curtains/ the curtains are white/ real white curtains and his skin is blue/ black against them. His eyes are wide, real wide. He's holding his comics/ I'm holding mine and we just stare at each other. It seems like an eternity, the staring. Two young boys with comic books/ like any boys/ anywhere. The next day in school, Alton and I ignored each other. There was no great event. We just stopped speaking.

ALMA. It's Saturday, I get up early to slop the hogs, feed the chickens and rake the yard so I can watch "The Monkees" and "Kookla, Fran and Ollie." I'm inside the house. I hear Odelia *(Odelia.)* "JOHN!" *(Alma.)* I look out and see a tall light-skinned man. He walks slowly up to the house — *(Odelia.)* "John — ooh baby — I so glad ta seeya — ohh baby I does missya — wanna see Alma — See yo baby." *(Alma.)* She throws her arms around his neck. He removes her arms and pats her on the head. He pats her on the head like a dog. He says *(John.)* "Where she at?" *(Alma.)* He had a Geechie accent like people from Russelville. I wonder if he is from Russelville but not too many light-skinned people live here. Again he says *(John.)* "Where she at?" *(Alma.)* Odelia yells/ roars *(Odelia.)* "ALMA/ ALMA COME OUT AN SEE YO DADDY!" *(Alma.)* I go and stand by the screen door. He — John

— "my father" says *(John.)* "Come on out heah gal!" *(Alma.)* I open the screen door and walk slowly towards him. He, "John" — my father — the man Odelia said had "purty yella skin" — lurches toward me smelling of gin. I know it's gin because Odelia smells the same way when she drinks it. *(John.)* "Damn she a big ole ting — she ain't as black as you but probably be big like you." *(Alma.)* His skin is red/ greasey/ shiny/ gin-filled. *(John.)* "Her face kinda long horse face like you. How I knows dis gal belong ta me?"

     (Odelia.) "Dis is yo baby John!" *(Alma.)* He says *(John.)* "Bitch you know how many head o' chillun I got — you know how many uhman I laid up wit? She jes anotha one ta me!" *(Alma.)* He looks at me again and walks off the porch into the yard on the mini dirt road and then on to the tar road. Odelia runs after him. *(Odelia.)* "Don leave me — Alma, Alma, she yo baby — she yo baby!" *(Alma.)* She's running with her short nappy hair sticking up, her large, loose, defeated breasts swinging side to side. This tall, big dark woman close to six feet tall. She grabs me under one arm and runs down into the yard onto the dirt road and then hits the tar road. Her thick, bare feet hit the tar road. The soles of her bare feet are beating against the tar road — the hot tar road. *(Odelia.)* "DON'T GO!" *(Alma.)* She drops me — drops me like a sack of potatoes or corn. She reaches him and drops to her knees. *(Odelia.)* "Please John" — *(Alma.)* Grabs him around the ankles. *(Odelia.)* "Please John!" *(Alma.)* He grabs her by her nappy hair and yanks her head back. *(John.)* "Bitch I ain't ga neva love you." *(Alma.)* He walks down the road. I go over to her and she pushes me away. I say "Come on — let's go back!" She pushes me away panting. She lay on the hot tar road panting — panting like a dog.

     Odelia drinks heavily that night. She drinks almost an entire bottle of gin. *(Odelia.)* "Why ya born ta me? Why ya run John off?" *(Alma.)* She staggers over to me, slaps me. She makes up a "love root." She sometimes sold love roots to women who wanted to catch men. She says to me gin-filled *(Odelia.)* "I ga get a root to make ya lighter. I ga put it in yo food — an EAT IT — YA BETTA EAT IT!" EUGENE. I tell Momma what happened with Alton. She's filled up on Bourbon. *(Thelma.)* "Vera Mae White spoke to you like that?" *(Eugene.)* "Yeah Momma. Why did she say that to me? I didn't do anything."

ALMA. *(Odelia.)* "EAT it — If ya was light, John woulda been heah."

EUGENE. Momma tells daddy *(Thelma.)* "That tramp Vera Mae you ran with years ago attacked Eugene — " *(Robert.)* "I went with her because your father wouldn't let me date you. When people in your family didn't want me around. She and I came from the same place. She understood — she understood things you and Eugene will never understand" —

ALMA. "It don't taste good — it's nasty!" — *(Odelia.)* "EAT IT!" *(Alma.)* At the end of the week, I am still the same color and the same size. That Friday night Odelia fills up on gin. She pulls me out of bed yelling *(Odelia.)* "Damn you! Damn you! — "

EUGENE. *(Thelma.)* "I gave up my family to marry you. What more do you want? How long do I have to suffer because you're dark — I don't care about that — how long have I told you this — I CHOSE YOU — I LOVE YOU!"

ALMA. Odelia holds my head under water. I'm gasping for air. She does this three times. She dries me off, combs and braids my hair then puts me to bed —

EUGENE. *(Robert.)* "Baby I'm sorry, I know you gave up everything for me — I know. Nobody ever loved me like that — Nobody never loved ME." *(Eugene.)* He speaks softly to Momma but never to me.

ALMA. I dream of Odelia panting on the highway. Her tongue is long — like a dog's. I get on my knees and look skyward. "Why God — how come You made me so dark and big? Please God, I wanna be light so Daddy can come back. I wanna be small and not take up a whole buncha space."

EUGENE. Momma collapses and he — Daddy — leads her into their bedroom —

ALMA. "I don't wanna be dark an big — make me pretty God — make me light and pretty! — "

EUGENE. I hear their voices — his voice low — from the belly — from the gut —

ALMA. "I don't wanna be on a road breathing like a dog — If you can't make me light and small, could you please come and take me? — "

EUGENE. Her voice is high — high and Momma like —

ALMA. "I don't want nobody to leave me on no road like a dog — If I can't be light an small, I don't wanna be here anymore — "
EUGENE. Momma moans/ screams — and calls "Oh God — oh God! — "
ALMA. "Please God — come an take me wit you — "
EUGENE. Daddy's voice rumbles "Goddamn — Goddamn!" — my daddy curses God —
ALMA. God —
EUGENE. They are hurting each other. Her high voice — his low voice — one seems is crying — the other grunting. I lie on my bed trying to sleep — it's a summer day — I'm not supposed to be sleeping — it's summer. I pretend Alton and Alma and I are in my room —
ALMA. *(Singing.)* Here we come —
EUGENE. On your mark — get set — go —
ALMA. *(Still singing.)* Walking down the street —
EUGENE. Let's put our arms to the side —
ALMA. *(Singing.)* "We get the funniest looks from everyone we meet — hey, hey we're the Monkees —
EUGENE. Come on run, run fast, you can do it.
BOTH. *(Singing.)* "People say we monkey around — we're too busy singin to put anybody down."

PART II

ALMA. My body is changing — doing things I knew about/ heard about but can't understand — I'm fourteen —

EUGENE. I'm dreaming of wanting to touch and be touched —

ALMA. I'm getting dressed and Odelia comes into my room and takes one look at me and grins." *(Odelia.)* "Oh ya getting up dere now. We gots ta git ya a trainin bra — "

EUGENE. I'm staring at all these girls — I'm aware of them — I'm aware of them physically — so much so it is overwhelming. I am sixteen. I'm sixteen thinking I'm gonna die if I don't touch a girl. I'm aware of the way they smell — the sweat that is on their skin and how it mingles with them — how it mingles with themselves and rises to the surface —

ALMA. "Trainin' bra? — what am I trainin' for? — "

EUGENE. Wyce and I are "boys." *(Pause.)* Alton and I are long gone — our days of being friends are gone. So Wyce and I are "tight" — are "boys" and we check out girls together. *(Wyce.)* "I fucked this bitch last night, man — had her screamin ALL night long. See that girl over there, man? Man, she wanted to get down with me but I didn't want her, man — she ain't fine enough for me." *(Eugene.)* I knew he was lying but it's okay — it's okay because we're "boys" — we are each other's "boy." Wyce — he says *(Wyce.)* "My boy Gene!" —

ALMA. So Odelia buys me this "training bra" and begins to monitor my looks. *(Odelia.)* "Alma you don be need to be eatin all dat candy, you an no lil chile — ya fourteen years old — ya big enough as it is — "

EUGENE. I'm looking at all kinds of girls — dark, light, skinny — not too skinny — and big, not too big mind you. Wyce always looks at thin light-skinned girls. If I point out a girl that is bigger or darker and go "Man, don't you think that girl is fine?" he looks at me and says, *(Wyce.)* "Gene are you crazy?"

ALMA. I'm fourteen — I have these budding breasts but I'm still fourteen. Blood fills me then leaves me every month but I'm still fourteen. I am supposed to eat candy.

EUGENE. I begin to look at Alma differently. Once we were talking and I accidentally brushed against her breast. *(To her.)* "I'm sorry" but I really wasn't.

ALMA. He touches my breast by accident and then he looks me in the face —

EUGENE. I'm aware of how soft her breast is — how warm it is —

ALMA. I want him to touch me. I can't look him back in the face but I want him to touch me.

EUGENE. I want to kiss her breasts.

ALMA. He'll be the only one to ever touch me.

EUGENE. *(Wyce.)* "Eugene, man, I got us hooked up with some fine girls. We can get some wine and hang and party with them." *(Eugene.)* So my boy Wyce introduces me to these very fine girls. Wyce and I, we're dancing, drinking, partying with these very fine light-skinned girls —

ALMA. I don't want anybody but Gene.

EUGENE. I start making out with this girl — this fair girl with real long hair —

ALMA. Wyce and Gene are hanging with these light-skinned guys and they always have light-skinned girls with them — these girls with long swinging hair that they — the light-skinned boys — play with or they — the girls — are always running their hands through thinking they're so cute, throwing their heads back to get the hair out of their faces. Sometimes the hair does not land on their faces or in their eyes — they throw back their heads for show — just to show how long their hair is — just for show.

EUGENE. We're drinking wine from my parents' bar. I don't like the way it tastes but I like the way it makes me feel. The girl drinks from my glass — her lips are wet and thin —

ALMA. I hate light-skinned girls —

EUGENE. I'm making out with this girl and I look down at this girl and say "Damn you are fine!" *(Pause.)* Oh, she is — she is sooo fine. Wyce is on the other side making out with her friend and says *(Wyce.)* "Yo Gene ain't this sweet, man!" *(Eugene.)* and I say, "Yo Wyce, this is real sweet — "

ALMA. All LIGHT-SKINNED GIRLS ARE BITCHES!

EUGENE. The girl is sweet and fine but Alma is sweet and fine to me — I want this girl to be Alma. I kiss this girl's breasts thinking of Alma's breasts —

ALMA. I worry about the light-skinned girls that are hanging around. I tell Odelia that I'm worried. She says *(Odelia.)* "Ya see? I had told ya 'bout dem high yella/ red bitches." *(Alma.)* I say "Eugene never asked me to be his girl." *(Odelia.)* "Dat boy does like ya an ya ga haveta find a way to catch him fore one o'dem yella girls snatch him way from ya — "

EUGENE. I'm on top of this girl and I'm riding her — I'm not making love — I'm just riding her —

ALMA. I want Gene but I'm not going to dog-pant — pant like a dog. *(Beat.)*

EUGENE. I just keep riding the girl — this is my first time and I'm riding. I'm not looking at her — my eyes are closed and I've got wine — now bourbon coursing through me. I open my eyes and say, "I don't want no high yella women — yeah you look good but I don't want anything high yellow." The girl looks at me horrified. I go home and call Alma and tell her about the girl —

ALMA. I fill up on hate — totally fill up on hate. I close my eyes and see them kissing. I close my eyes and see these two butter colored people kissing. *(To Eugene.)* "Is her hair long? — "

EUGENE. *(To Alma.)* "Her hair is long. When I was with her I ran my hands through her hair — "

ALMA. I touch my hair. I touch my short, nappy hair. I push back tears — I push them way back. I will not dog-pant —

EUGENE. *(To Alma.)* "Wyce set me up with this girl and we hung out. It didn't mean anything. You know the girl/ you've seen her around."

ALMA. The following week I see her in St. Stephen with her mother. I watch her as she walks. Her hair swings and caresses her back as she walks. I want to cut off all her hair/ I want to rip her hair from the root/ I want to cut her across her face but her mother's there. Her mother smiles at me and says hello. The girl then looks at me and smiles — a real smile, a friendly smile. She smiles wanting to connect — I look at her and realize that she knows nothing about me and Gene. She smiles a real smile, a genuine smile. She and her mother. I almost smile back — almost. Then I think of Eugene and her kissing. I think of them kissing and it burns me.

EUGENE. Wyce and I are in my backyard drinking/ smoking. *(Wyce.)* "Man, I can't believe you said you didn't like light women. What's wrong with you? Hey you feel guilty for bein' light? You see how darker dudes have always called us pussies." *(Eugene.)* "Man I don't know why I said it. I don't know." *(Wyce.)* "I don't feel bad about bein light, man, and I ain't gonna let no darkassed Geechie mess with me. *(Pause.)* For instance notice how your friend Alton White hasn't been around lately?"

(Eugene.) I look at Wyce and get a chill. "Yo, Wyce. What did you do, man?" *(Wyce.)* "Naw, I put that dude in his place, man. That nigga/ Geechie spook got all big and bad." *(Eugene.)* "What did you DO Wyce?" *(Wyce.)* "You know how he was trying to sell those two puppies of his?" *(Eugene.)* "Yeah." *(Wyce.)* "Well, let's just say I helped him out. I see him — Alton — and I say 'Hey bro, what's up?' and he looks at me — fucking white of his eyes — ugly blackassed nigga lookin at me." *(Alton.)* "I ain't none o' ya bro, ole red punk nigga."

(Wyce.) "Gene, I'm looking at this nigga tryin not to laugh — Yo, man can't you see how black and ugly he is? *(Frowns.)* — Goddamn. *(Beat.)* Anyway I say 'I think all of us need to stop this 'cause all of us got to get together. All of us are black no matter what and we shouldn't be holdin each otha down.' *(Wyce begins to laugh.)* Gene this nigga starts grinning and I say 'Yo, Alton, why don't I come after school to check out the puppies you sellin?' and he's saying *(Alton.)* 'Yeah, Wyce, yeah bro.' *(Wyce.)* So during recess, I bum a Kool cigarette off somebody and give to him and he's thinking that we're tight, right? I mean this boy swears WE ARE TIGHT. So after school we go to his house and the two puppies are in the yard and I reach for the dark one — Midnight — of course the black one is named Midnight — and I play with him and I say 'Yo, Alton let's take a walk.' So we walk past Georgia Pacific and we turn down the dirt road near Alma's house and we walk towards some Geechie juke joint — all these nonworking pitchblack motherfuckers with no job hanging around drinkin beer and listenin to some old time music. We walk past this shit hole and I say 'You know Alton, I changed my mind. I don't want

to buy this dog and I don't want to be your friend — UGLY BLACKASSED NIGGA.' He goes to jump on me but I jump back still holding the dog and I reach for my pocket knife and Alton begins to drool. *(Laughs.)* I mean this black motherfucker is drooling, man. I hold the dog up and slit its throat — I slit it slow and easy man and I say — calm, cool, collected — I say 'You and this dog look a lot alike except that you're living and it's dead. If you ever call me a punk again or get bad with me, I'll do you just like this dog.'" *(Beat. Eugene.)* I make an excuse to get Wyce to leave — I can't be around him — I have to see Alma. *(Alma and Eugene speak their thoughts aloud:)*

ALMA. "Gene I'm afraid. I get afraid a lot — I don't want to hate anybody Gene — "

EUGENE. Alma's the best person I know.

ALMA. "People think because I'm bigger and darker that I have all the answers — "

EUGENE. The kids always say "Man Alma ain't nobody to mess with — "

ALMA. "But I get confused all the time — "

EUGENE. Wyce won't say so but I know he's afraid of her —

ALMA. "What I want to say is, can you take care of me Gene? Can you make me feel pretty? Do you think I take up too much space?"

EUGENE. I wish I could touch her.

ALMA. "I'm afraid you'll make me dog-pant."

EUGENE. Not just kiss her — touch her — REALLY touch her.

ALMA. His shoulders are broad — his teeth are even — even teeth under thin lips —

EUGENE. I kiss her — I kiss her and she tastes sweet — more than sweet — she tastes CLEAN —

ALMA. So he puts his tongue in my mouth. It's not like I think it would be — It feels funny — this tongue in my mouth — somebody else's tongue in my mouth —

EUGENE. I'm beginning to relax — I'm beginning to relax because Alma's holding me —

ALMA. He tastes like wine or beer and gum —

EUGENE. I smell/ feel her sweat and she tastes good — She's clean — so clean —

21

ALMA. I think I like it — being kissed — I think I do — Is this all there is to being kissed?
EUGENE. She's so strong — real strong. Kissing Alma, I was home — I knew I was finally home.

PART III

ALMA. Graduation day is just around the corner. I doubled up on my credits to graduate early. I'm seventeen and — walking pretty. I'm starting to walk pretty. I get a job in Woolworth's for the summer. I begin to get my hair straightened and buy makeup. When people come in the store, they notice and say, "Alma you look just like new money." I'm seventeen and I'm floating down St. Stephen's streets reading about New York and other places, buying lipstick — pursing my lips with lipsticks bearing fruit names like "Wildberry" or "Boysenberry." I paint my eyelids with "Angel Blue" eyeshadow and "Come Hither" green. I'm seventeen — hear my voice — watch me walk.

EUGENE. I'm in my room listening to music and Daddy comes in. *(Robert.)* "Well, Gene, graduation day is almost here — what plans do you have?" *(Eugene.)* "Well, what do you mean "what plans," daddy?" *(Robert.)* "What do you want to do with your life?" *(Eugene.)* "I don't know Daddy." *(Robert.)* "Eugene, you're nineteen years old and don't know what to do with your life — you're pathetic — you really are."

ALMA. I hear Odelia's voice shooting me down. Trying to shoot shoot — shoot me down. She's trying to shoot down my new walk/ talk. She says *(Odelia.)* "Wearin all dat ole mess on ya face an still don't look lak nuttin — you ain't NEVA gon look lak nuttin/ you neva gon look good." *(Alma.)* I turn on her/ I shoot her down, "Yeah but I betcha I ain't neva ran behin no man dog-pantin an beggin him to stay like you, ain't it?" I shudder, hearing my/ her Gullah Geechie voice. I shudder.

EUGENE. The week before graduation Momma says, *(Thelma.)* "Eugene, my father would like to meet you." *(Eugene.)* I'm stunned because I knew he cut her off for marrying Daddy. I say, "After what he put you through — after the way he treated you and Daddy?" *(Thelma.)* "He's a strong man who stuck by what he felt. He worked hard to provide for me and he gave up a lot. My

23

daddy didn't have any kind of help from his family. His father left them and he had to help support the family. He didn't have the education he should have — can't you see that? People saw him as high yellow trash. White people hated him and other black people too — and I hate to say it Gene — darker skinned people really hurt him — he suffered Gene. He can't help the way he is. I want you to see him — YOU ARE GOING TO SEE HIM. He's still my daddy and your grandaddy and I love him."

ALMA. Her-Odelia's voice is rough, slack — the vowels that are present are slurry, lost in her throat — with or without gin they are slurry and lost in her throat.

EUGENE. I ask Momma, "Why does he want to see me?" She can't look me in the eye. She says, *(Thelma.)* "I sent a picture of you and he sent a message back saying it was okay for you to visit him — "

ALMA. I will not let the words get lost or slurry in my throat — I want my voice to be clear — heard. I hear her and I hear my own voice. I CANNOT STAND MY VOICE —

EUGENE. So I go visit him — "this man" — my "grandfather" — my blood/ kin. I drive there slowly, my eyes alternately looking at the road and the clock. I don't want to get there too early nor do I want to be there late. I park the car and walk up to his — my grandaddy's porch and I ring the bell. My heart is in my mouth — it feels like my heart is in my mouth. I hear him inside walking towards the door and I break into a sweat. He opens the door and we stare at each other — we're standing there, both our mouths slightly open. We're looking at the old/ young versions of each other —

ALMA. I look at her — Odelia's body. I look at her body and see what my body will become. I look at her and see that it will become thick and wide.

EUGENE. We continue to stare and finally he — Grandaddy Eugene invites me in to his house — a house filled with furniture — antique furniture and light — his house is filled with light and darkness. It's strange how his house is both light and dark. He leads me into his parlor and appraises me —

ALMA. I think how I can use Eugene's voice. I cannot change THE BODY — *(Pause.)* MY BODY *(Pause.)* but the voice. I can make my voice sound like Gene's. I can take his inflections and rhythm. I can listen to the gentle way he pronounces his S's and T's. I can make the R's sound like honey in my throat. I can take from the books I read — the words in my head and the words in my throat — I can combine those words — I can have a new voice — My own voice —

EUGENE. Grandaddy smiles/ whispers *(Grandfather.)* "Look at you — O my God/ thank God — LOOK AT YOU." *(Eugene.)* All I can manage to say is "Yessir?" He — Grandaddy — leans over and touches my hair, strokes my face murmuring, *(Grandfather.)* "God — thank God — I can't believe it." *(Eugene.)* He keeps staring and I avert my eyes. I look up/ down and smile. He — keeps staring like he's hypnotized. *(Beat.)* I look at the objects in this room. I can't get over all the furniture and paintings and glassware. I recognize some of the glassware because Momma has some that matches it. He — Granddaddy — says *(Grandfather.)* "Like what you see son?" *(Eugene.)* "Yessir I do." *(Grandfather.)* "How does the world treat you, son?" *(Eugene.)* "I don't understand, sir — what do you mean?" He pulls his chair close to me. *(Beat. Grandfather.)* "The world can be hard on us/ people like us." *(Eugene.)* "What do you mean *people like us*? I don't know what you mean." *(Grandfather.)* "The white man hates us/ dark-skinned niggers hate us. *(Pause.)* NOW do you know what I mean? *(Pause. Softly.)* YOU DO know what I mean. YOU DO/ I can see it/ You do know." *(Eugene. Confused.)* "Well I don't really think about it — I guess maybe sometimes I get razzed but — " *(Grandfather.)* "I hope you fight back. It's not the crackers you have to worry about — it's them darkassed Geechies. I hope you don't let them push you around." *(Eugene.)* "Well I deal with it and it's a little tense sometimes — but I handle it." *(Grandfather.)* "I'm telling you NOT to let those bastards push you around. Don't let ANY of the black sons o' bitches think they can do you all kinds of ways. *(Beat.)* I knew you were catching hell when I saw the picture of you/ amazing what a picture can do. Now you're sitting here confirming it. *(Beat.)* Let me tell you something — listen to me because I know what you're going through and I'm trying to tell you not to let the bastards do it to you/ LISTEN TO ME/ LEARN FROM ME/ I KNOW WHAT YOU'RE GOING

THROUGH/ I'VE BEEN THROUGH IT. *(Beat.)* So do you have a girlfriend?" *(Eugene.)* "Yessir, I do." *(Grandfather.)* "Is it serious?" *(Eugene.)* "Well, yessir it is." *(Grandfather.)* "Don't you think you're a little young to be getting serious?" *(Eugene.)* "Well, no sir, I don't think so." *(Grandfather.)* "You should be sowing your oats — Listen sow your oats but do me one favor son." *(Eugene.)* He calls me "son." *(Grandfather.)* "If you wanna mess with something dark that's fine but DON'T MARRY NOTHIN DARK." *(Eugene.)* "Well, sir I don't really see it that way. Light or dark — it makes no difference to me." *(Grandfather.)* "Boy you really are silly — Don't you know them darkassed Geechies think we're punks — FAGGOTS because we're light? Nobody, I mean nobody, ever gave me nothing and I do mean nothing. I went to work at Georgia Pacific when I was fourteen, chopping lumber, stackin lumber — my hands all cut up and rough. I worked just as hard as anybody else but you couldn't tell that to them dark-skinned guys — no, they didn't believe that. It was always 'Ole yella nigga soft' or 'Hey red nigga, you ain't so big now' or 'Yeah it hot but the sweat jes run thru his haid — it don't git nappy — ain't you purty.' *(Pause.)* Always — all my life they did that to me. They thought I didn't struggle or sweat. They thought I had it so easy. *(Beat.)* One day one of them got in my face one day because his sister had a thing for me. I didn't pay her any mind but this nig-ger was just LOOKIN to get in my face. So this one day in the yard, he says to me 'Hey look ya, yo momma was suposeta be so fine lookin but yo Daddy still runoff ain't it?' And this bastard began to laugh. The sweat was dripping off of him and he and all of them started lookin at me laughin and I grabbed a hold of him and just started pounding. Right there in the lumber yard. We were fighting in the yard. The white foreman looked down at us laughing — laughing at the dark and light niggers going at it. *(Pause.)* I guess we gave him one helluva show. *(Pause.)* I threw some sawdust in his eyes and he fell to the ground moaning, screaming holding his eyes, 'I can't see, I can't see.' *(Pause.)* I blind-ed him — Oh yeah, he went blind. *(Beat.)* None of the darker men messed with me after that — none — but the hate was in their eyes. Their hate made me work harder — eventually I made it to foreman. I EARNED THAT JOB — GODDAMN, I

EARNED IT." *(Eugene.)* "I know you did, sir." *(Grandfather.)* "They never let them pitch black bastards be foremen in my day — NOT IN MY DAY — As soon as I saw your father that damned Robert coming, grinning up at those crackers, trying to put in for overtime I KNEW he was after my job. I knew what he was doing. I KNEW. Your father — *black bastard* — tried to take my job but he didn't take it. I retired — He saw I wasn't some high/yella punk — I retired." *(Eugene.)* "Don't you call my father a black bastard!" *(Pause.)* He looks at me giving me a look I recognize as my own. I walk out. I walk out recognizing the look as my own. I walk out shaking, afraid — realizing how I could hurt someone. I recognized the hate in his eyes and saw my own. I saw my own hate. *(Beat.)*

ALMA. Graduation day finally get here, the summer that was so unbearably hot becomes one of the best summers of my life.

EUGENE. My parents offer to have a graduation supper for us. Alma graduated early. She doubled up on her credits. She was very determined to graduate early and she did. Right after the graduation services I sneak a beer. Alma and Odelia are coming over for the first time. I just had to have it — the beer before supper.

ALMA. Odelia's running around *(Odelia.)* "Lawd — I gotta find me a purty dress — ooh — I excited — Lawd. Alma we goin ta dey house fa dinner — I can't hardly believe it — I got ta find me a pretty dress. Lawd you see how pretty Thelma is — huh skin lak butta — lawd help me find da right dress!"

EUGENE. Momma cooks a feast. Yams, turkey, greens, sweet potatoes. She's wearing a pretty off-white dress. She's sitting by her makeup table with a glass of bourbon. She looks at me through the mirror smiling as she's making herself up. *(Thelma.)* "How do I look baby?" *(Eugene.)* "Fine Momma." She hands her glass to me and says *(Thelma.)* "Freshen Momma's drink baby — "

ALMA. *(Odelia.)* "I gotta git me a lil gin to calm my nerves. I gots da perfume — yeah dis perfume outta Woolworth but it nice — it nice even though it from there and mah flower — gotta put mah flower in dis ole nappy head o' mine — Does I look good Alma?"

EUGENE. I pick up Alma and Odelia and bring them to the house. Momma shows Odelia around —

ALMA. *(Odelia.)* "Looka da curtains an pictures an furniture an tings. Looka all dis silvaware — I ain't neva see such silva and things — looka da way you fix da table all nice like — I so glad you had us to come heah — an looka dat hair o' yourn Thelma — so long an purty — chile ya got dat long, good hair — Ain't she go nice hair Alma?" *(Alma.)* "Yes I guess so." Thelma looks at me. I look at her. The corner of her mouth is smiling but somehow held tight.

EUGENE. I'm watching Alma look at Odelia. "Don't be too hard on her Alma."

ALMA. I'm watching Mr. Gaines watch Odelia. I can see the look of disgust in his eyes. I can see him looking at her thinking "I made it out of Russelville — why didn't you?" He's looking at her thinking "You stupid, hungry backwoods bitch."

EUGENE. *(To Alma.)* "Odelia really is sweet." Odelia tries to talk about people she and Daddy grew up with.

ALMA. *(Odelia.)* "Looka heah Robert, do you rememba — "

EUGENE. *(Robert.)* "Odelia — I never dealt with those people. I was working and in school full-time."

ALMA. Odelia's doing most of the talking — getting drunker and stupider by the minute holding this champagne glass — *(Odelia.)* "Ain't this gloriable like?" *(Alma.)* She downs the champagne quickly, wipes her mouth with the back of her hand, grinning — grinning a Stephin Fetchit grin. She then reaches for the gin glass. In my head I pray "God, let me disappear."

EUGENE. Daddy keeps staring hard at Odelia but he keeps filling her gin glass. He fills his and Momma's bourbon glasses as well. He can see that she's far gone but keeps filling her glass. I try to make a joke of it, "Well, I guess Odelia is feeling pretty fine — "

ALMA. I'm looking at Thelma who's also drunk. Her light skin is now ruddy from bourbon. She says —

EUGENE. *(Thelma.)* "You look nice tonight Alma."

ALMA. "Thank you." *(Odelia.)* "Thelma, you know you a little tipsy. You just as red as you can be." *(To Alma.)* "Alma, maybe you and Gene *can* make some purty yella babies." *(Silence.)*

EUGENE. The silence is loud, piercing at the table —

ALMA. I get up — I have to — I have to get up and shake that room. I get up and say "I would like very much to make an announcement." I take a sip of champagne. I look over at Odelia who's grinning that ridiculous grin. I look at her with this fake flower in her hair which is now lopsided — I look at her with her legs now spread wide apart and know she thinks I'm going to announce that me and Gene are getting married. I look her in the face and say, "I've been accepted to Hunter College in New York City in the fall with full financial aid and I'm going."

EUGENE. I feel my mouth going dry. I turn to Daddy. "Excuse me sir. I know that drinking age isn't until you're twenty-one but I really could use a shot of bourbon right now."

ALMA. I look over at Gene — he avoids my eyes —

EUGENE. Daddy says *(Robert.)* "Alma you are really going places — you're taking the bull by the horns — good for you."

ALMA. Thelma looks at me —

EUGENE. *(Thelma.)* "Oh how nice — "

ALMA. She looks at me thin-lipped/ tight-lipped — glad I'm going —

EUGENE. Daddy looks at me and says, *(Robert.)* "Well, Gene. Wyce is joining the service and Alma's going up north. It seems like everybody is passing you by."

ALMA. Mr. Gaines says, *(Robert.)* "Alma, you're just like me — you're making something of yourself. You and I know what it's like to struggle." *(Alma.)* He goes to the bar and gets the bottles of bourbon and gin and puts them on the table. He refills his glass yet again and he pats my knee. His hand lingers — I push his hand away —

EUGENE. I pour a big drink, down it and quickly pour another. Now I understand why people drink —

ALMA. Eugene drives Odelia and me home. As soon as Gene drives off she yells, *(Odelia.)* "WHO YA THINK YA IS — DAT BOY GA LEAVE YA AN GIT HIM A PURTY LIGHT-SKINNED GIRL — YA FAT FILTHY UGLY BLACK BITCH!" *(Alma.)* She goes to the cabinet and pours a very large gin into the jelly/ glass jar and downs it. She can barely stand. She can barely stand but goes to hit me. I grab her arm — I grab her arm bringing her to her knees — I bring her all the way down to her knees and say "You're right. I am ugly, big, dark but if you want me to take care of you — if you ever want to, as you say, 'live good,' don't you EVER put your hands on me again, I'll make sure you never

29

come near me and Gene and that you live here for the rest of your UGLY BLACK life."

EUGENE. I go to Alma's house the next day. "You didn't say anything about New York to me — "

ALMA. "I talk about it constantly. Eugene let's leave here — New York seems so great."

EUGENE. "You just mentioned New York — you didn't seem serious — I always thought we'd stay here, together."

ALMA. "We've got nothing really keeping us here — "

EUGENE. "You're just a little restless. You'll settle down and it will be fine and we"ll make a life here. We"ll get a house and live in St. Stephen — "

ALMA. "I want to see Manhattan — I hear it's huge — "

EUGENE. "What is the big deal about New York?"

ALMA. "I'm not going to slop hogs and rake chicken shit. I have to make something of my self Gene — I HAVE TO BE SOMEBODY — "

EUGENE. "You are somebody — "

ALMA. "I am nobody — nothing — I am nothing — "

EUGENE. "You're being silly Alma — "

ALMA. "I am not being silly — "

EUGENE. "You start reading about New York and dreaming all this crazy stuff. Wanting to live so high and mighty and no matter what, you'll still be a country girl from South Carolina — "

ALMA. *(Incensed.)* "Yeah says the rich boy — easy for you to say. You try getting up and slopping hogs, feeding chickens, raking the yard, before school — "

EUGENE. *(Apologetic.)* "Alma — I didn't mean — "

ALMA. "Try having to get up earlier to do all that as well as clean the house and then make breakfast and supper — "

EUGENE. "Alma — I'm sorry — "

ALMA. "Not to mention having to use the outhouse — having to get up and go outside in the middle of the night. You know NOTHING about having to fill a tin tub to wash clothes in and to bathe in — YOU NEVER had to do that! I have to squeeze myself in a tin tub to take a bath Gene — Do I want to take a shower and use an inside bathroom and bathe in a real tub — LIKE YOU — do I want to live like you — Yes — I do. I am not

30

rich, or light or live in the city limits but I will be a somebody —
I am going to be a somebody BECAUSE I WANT MORE — "

EUGENE. "I've always said we'd live in the city limits. *(Beat.)*
Why did you say 'I'm not rich or light?' — why did you have to say
that Alma?"

ALMA. *(Quietly.)* "Because it's true — "

EUGENE. "You didn't have to say that Alma." *(They both are
quiet for a minute.)* "Do you really feel you need to go to New
York? Do you really have to go?"

ALMA. "I have to go." *(Beat.)*

EUGENE. Daddy gets me a job at Georgia Pacific — the work is
tough. I'm chopping, lifting lumber — my hands are getting cut —
The heat is unbearable — "Daddy, it's really hot. I'd like to get some
water." *(Robert.)* "Stop calling me Daddy — you call me SIR."

ALMA. I buy these summer dresses to go to work in — I know
I'm only working in a Woolworth's but I want to look nice —

EUGENE. Some of the guys I went to school with are working
in the lumberyard — the dark-skinned guys are working in the
lumberyard. *(Voices.)* "Ole pretty yella nigga can't handle the heat."
"Soft yella bitch." "Pretty, yella and soft." *(Beat. Eugene.)* Daddy
laughs along with the dark-skinned guys.

ALMA. I'm also putting money aside for fall clothes — I never
really had to think about that, fall clothes, clothes for the "fall"
— I look forward to wearing "fall" clothes — I look forward to
the "fall."

EUGENE. I mention Alma's leaving to Wyce. He says *(Wyce.)*
"Man, I hear when bitches get up there to new York, they hook up
with some of those dudes up there and TOTALLY forget about the
South — they get NEW YORK fever, man."

ALMA. Odelia says *(Odelia.)* "Wastin money buyin all dat mess.
Some o' dat money could come in heah to dis house." *(Alma.)* I
look down and at her and say "This money is going towards
school and NOTHING else."

EUGENE. *(Beat.)* I'm watching her change. She no longer has
the Geechie accent. She's wearing makeup, straightening her hair
and bought these clothes. I've never seen her look this good. I
mean she ALWAYS looks good to me but now she's looking beautiful — she's looking incredibly beautiful. She's looking like this

31

about to leave me — Next thing I know the summer is gone and I'm taking Alma to the train.

ALMA. As we're driving, I notice how different Russelville is looking already —

EUGENE. She's chattering away about the dorm room and how she hopes she and her roommate get along —

ALMA. We get to the station. We have a little time before the train comes. We start kissing. I pull away and say "You taste like liquor — "

EUGENE. "I had to steady my nerves." My nerves were shot —

ALMA. We continue to kiss — we kiss — long, hard, deep —

EUGENE. She's looking beautiful and kissing me like she never kissed me before. She's holding me close — real close, running her hands down my back —

ALMA. The train gets here. We put my bags on the train and kiss some more. The train pulls away and Eugene is running with the train blowing kisses like they do in the movies —

EUGENE. I run and run and run —

ALMA. I'm wearing full makeup — I'm wearing one of my pretty dresses fully made up —

EUGENE. I keep running until I can't run any more —

ALMA. I'm applying, reapplying lipstick, putting on different colors —

EUGENE. I watch the train until it totally disappears —

ALMA. Odelia cooked a tremendous amount of food — all this fried chicken, cake, there was a thermos of iced tea. The conductor walks by and asks, *(Conductor.)* "Young lady did your mother fry a lot of chicken for you?" I say, *(Alma.)* "Yessir — how did you know?" He says, *(Conductor.)* "You passengers call it the 'iron express' but we call it the 'chicken bone' express!'

EUGENE. I walk back to the car —

ALMA. I decide to go to the "cocktail" car — I hear this expression on the train. "Cocktail." Someone says "I'm going to the 'cocktail car.' What did I know about somebody's cocktail? But I didn't care — I wanted to have a 'cocktail.'

EUGENE. I get in the car and reach over into the glove compartment —

ALMA. I order a "white wine." I don't know but I feel that I

should have a "white wine — "
EUGENE. I pull out the bourbon —
ALMA. I'm sipping this cheap awful tasting stuff —
EUGENE. I bring it to my lips —
ALMA. But — it's my first grown-up drink and I'm enjoying it. It doesn't matter that it's cheap —
EUGENE. I bring my head back and take a long pull from the bottle —
ALMA. I'm sipping this cheap wine and feeling beautiful, grown-up and glorious —
EUGENE. I bring my head way back — way, way back —
ALMA. I feel beautiful — I am on this train riding — I am riding and I feel beautiful — I am beautiful. This white wine is the equivalent of the most glorious champagne and I am beautiful —
EUGENE. I take in this "taste" — this long taste of bourbon. I drive home. Daddy and Momma are sitting at the bar. You could see they've been there for a while. Daddy looks at me and says *(Robert.)* "Alma's gone?" *(Eugene.)* "Yeah, yeah she is." *(Robert.)* "Boy, people really are passing you by." *(Eugene.)* I yell "LEAVE ME ALONE! — LEAVE ME THE FUCK ALONE!" *(Robert.)* "Failure — YOU'RE NOTHING BUT A FAILURE!" *(Eugene.)* Momma starts in on the crying and I go upstairs to my room. I want to have a drink but not with them. So I'm in the room waiting. Daddy continues to yell at me from the bar. *(Robert.)* "FAILURE. YOU — YOU'RE A NOTHING." *(Eugene.)* I put the radio on and I then hear Momma crying and slurring. I can smell her upstairs. Jim Beam and Chanel Number Five wafting through the house. She's crying/ wailing. I turn the radio up a little higher. After a while, it gets quiet and I go to the top of the stairs and peep down. Momma cries/ slurs, *(Thelma.)* "Why can't you and Gene get along/ why can't you an my daddy get along — all of you are tearing me apart." *(Eugene.)* Daddy moves from around the bar and comes behind her. With his left hand he puts a filled glass of bourbon to her lips. He takes his right hand and slips it under her blouse caressing her right breast. She takes a drink and tongue smacks/ kisses the air. She is darting her tongue in the air. Her tongue doesn't connect with his. She's far gone — she doesn't know. He leads her — with his hand still on her breast to their

bedroom and closes the door. I hear her voice — high — high in her throat. I hear his voice — low and rumbling from his gut. I stand there for a good ten minutes and realize that they'll be in there for the rest of the night. I go down to the bar and pour a big stiff drink. I look down at my shirt and see Alma's lipstick. I down the drink and quickly pour another. I just sit there thinking and drinking. I sit there — me and Jim Beam.

PART IV

ALMA. I'm walking, talking, breathing New York. I've been here six months and I feel like I own it — it's mine. I've begun to wear high heels. I like the way my hips move in them. The clicking on the pavement along with the movement of my hips makes me feel sexy. When I'm walking — when my heels hit the pavement in Harlem, Chinatown — the Village, midtown — I feel sexy — my hips sway to the rhythm — the various rhythms of different neighborhoods — different streets. I try to explain this to Gene but I can't. I need him to come up and see it — See how I feel. See how I now walk/ see how I now move. In Harlem, I walk to a Southern beat — various Southern beats. I do it Northern style. Slick, clean, fast, Northern style. Sometimes it's like walking/ dancing to Robert Johnson and Otis Redding. Other times — it's harder/ faster — more dangerous — like a Parliament/ Funkadelic song. When my heels click in El Barrio, it's like walking/ dancing/ swirling to Tito Puente and Hector Lavoe. In Chinatown — I hear music where I don't know the name of musicians but am aware of a different rhythm — a rhythm filled with the sounds of bells and chants and my heels click to that — they can click to that — my hips move — differently but gently to that. I am moving in different kinds of weather — not just Southern heat. I am no longer barefoot in Southern heat in a dirt yard. I've adapted myself to the fall — the NEW YORK fall and the big sweaters that come with the fall. I am full booted and bundled for New York falls and winters. My hips are swaying — not just to the rhythm of Southern back door men. My hips are moving now by themselves free, uncontrolled and spontaneously. *(Beat.)* When my Trinidadian roommate tells me about her home, I can see the trees and West Indian women talking and laughing on porches. When in class, my teachers — who are in fact more than teachers — my guides — when my guides give my fellow students and me book assignments, I can via those words, see Dickens' London. I can see

35

Gogol's Russia. When I'm in the Museum of Modern Art, I can smell Georgia O'keefe's paint. In the Apollo theater, I can see/ hear Billie wailing, James Brown sweating, Marvin and Tammi teasing each other and teasing us. In the Village, I feel the rhythm of the pavement where Bob Dylan and Hendrix walked. *(Pause.)* I never knew how full life could be — it is so full. How expansive everything is outside of South Carolina. I cannot walk that walk anymore — that thick heeled, crusty, hot Southern dirt road walk — How could I possibly go back to that? I never knew I could enjoy the fullness of my walk — my hips. I can't wait to show this to Gene. How do you explain a new walk?

EUGENE. I tell Alma I'm coming up to visit. I'm dying to see her — I need to see her. I need to see "New York." I need to see these skyscrapers and subway stations. How big are the skyscrapers/ how long are the stations? I need to taste "Chinese/ Caribbean curries" she's always talking about — I want to see what's in those exotic stews. I want to taste them — I want to taste them with her. I want to see why she finds them so exotic and would I find them that way. I want to see/ hear the music she's always talking about. I cannot really hear/ have never heard anything much beyond gospel/ blues? Will I like anything beyond gospel/ blues? Is there anything beyond gospel/ blues? *(Beat.)* I take the train — my first train ride. *(Pause.)* I'm watching the trees as the train whizzes by. I'm aware how crooked they are. When I was a child they frightened me. I would look at those trees at night while I was in bed and think something would come through those trees and into the room and get me. But I'm looking out the window on my way to New York and I'm a grown man and it's daytime. *(Beat.)* An old woman across from me keeps offering me food. She tells me she's on her way to Philadelphia to visit her son. Next to her, there are two girls playing hand games. I look to my other side, there is a man quietly reading. All of these people have this look — this bearing — like they are so sure of everything. I hear one of the girls say, *(Little Girl 1.)* "I ain't never been to New York before but I'm glad I'm goin." *(Eugene.)* The other little girl says *(Little Girl 2.)* "Me too but I hear it's real bad." *(Eugene.)* Her sister says *(Little Girl 1.)* "We got to see for ourselves." *(Pause. Eugene.)* Out of the mouths of babes. *(Beat.)* How big is New York really/ Do people really get

"New York fever?" *(Beat.)* How could people live in a place so big without feeling lost? *(Pause.)* How do you not feel lost? *(Beat.)* I wonder how sleek/ slick some of those dudes are up there? Any of them hitting on Alma? I listen to Alma on the phone/ I listen to how different she sounds. She sounds like she's lived in New York forever. She doesn't ask about South Carolina at all — not at all. *(Beat.)* I can feel her holding me/ does she still WANT to hold me/ does she still WANT ME? *(Beat.)* I go to the "cocktail car." I have one bourbon — just one. I go back to my seat. The old lady is sleeping and so are the little girls. The man to my side is still reading. I look out the window and it's dark. The train keeps whizzing by those trees. Even though the train is moving fast, the trees still look scary, gloomy. I close my eyes — I will not look at the trees. Alma's holding me. I close my eyes — Alma and I are in New York and we're together.

ALMA. Gene gets here. I'm excited. He's finally here.

EUGENE. *(To Alma.)* "Here I am — New York city walking, talking, moving — "

ALMA. *(To Eugene.)* "South Carolina's still with you — still totally with you — still a part of you." *(They both pause.)*

EUGENE. "So it's been a long time — "

ALMA. "Yeah it has." *(They pause.)*

EUGENE. "Six months."

ALMA. "Six whole months." *(They pause. They look away from each other and there is another pause.)* I introduce him to my roommate and make reservations for dinner. *(Beat.)*

EUGENE. Alma's now wearing "New York" fashionable clothes — *(Beat.)*

ALMA. He looks nice. He's wearing nice clothes. You can tell he doesn't live in New York but he looks nice. *(Pause. Beat.)* I quickly change and we go to a great Chinese restaurant.

EUGENE. I don't know anything on the menu —

ALMA. I'm hoping he'll try things —

EUGENE. She's talking about her "psych course this" and her "sociology teacher" that —

ALMA. He's talking about people we went to school with — "This one had a baby with that person's husband" — *(Beat.)* he keeps looking at the menu. *(Pause.)* I order the food —

EUGENE. I'm eating this food that she says is so great. I mean it's okay. I could have easily eaten some American food — some soul food —

ALMA. He picks at the food — it's hard to get a reservation in this place — the food is that good.

EUGENE. I'm not crazy about New York but I see how comfortable she is here — she glides down the street — she more than walks — she glides — I'm watching her walk/ glide like she owns it. *(Beat.)* Man, I wish I had that walk —

ALMA. We walk through the Village. I say "Let's go dancing. I know a place with all kinds of great music."

EUGENE. I'm holding Alma close — real close — it's like being back in South Carolina. We start to kiss on the dance floor — my tongue/ her tongue —

ALMA. Eugene and I are dancing close/ he's holding me close — his hand is around my waist — he squeezes the flesh on my waist —

EUGENE. Alma's full, full body feels nice next to mine —

ALMA. My waist is fleshy — is there too much flesh on my waist?

EUGENE. I want to enter her/ be a part of her —

ALMA. I get a glimpse of myself in the club mirror. I see myself in this bar mirror —

EUGENE. I tell her, "I want to make love with you Alma — "

ALMA. I hear Odelia's voice, *(Odelia.)* "Big ole fat ting — ugly fat ting — ya lucky fa dat yella boy ta luv ya — Ain't nobody else ga love ya — "

EUGENE. "I love you Alma."

ALMA. I say "Love you too" — I feel myself breathing faster — I feel myself breathing faster and faster — I feel myself breathing like Odelia — I feel myself dog panting — panting like a dog —

EUGENE. I bring Alma back to the apartment I'm staying in —

ALMA. I sip some bourbon —

EUGENE. She's so nervous — "You're beautiful Alma — it's okay — "

ALMA. He removes my clothes — I look into the bedroom mirror, *(Odelia.)* "Fat ting — ole ugly black fat ting — "

EUGENE. I lay her on the bed — I touch her — I touch those warm breasts —

ALMA. How do I look against these sheets — how fat, black and

38

ugly do I look against these sheets? I tighten myself — I will make myself tight against these sheets.

EUGENE. I make love to her — I do it slow — I do not ride her — I make love to her.

ALMA. *(Odelia.)* "Fat ole ugly black ting — "

EUGENE. I'm inside of her — all the way inside of her —

ALMA. I'm being ripped apart — Part of me wants to melt/ glide into it — another part of me is being ripped apart — How do I look against the sheets?

EUGENE. It's okay — it's the first time —

ALMA. I'm being ripped apart — I'm bleeding — I'm being ripped apart for being a "fat black ugly" thing — I will not glide — I will not melt — I will not pant — *(Beat.)* I want to glide into this/ I want to melt into this —

EUGENE. I'm inside her — I want to always be inside her. "I love you Alma — I want to marry you — you're the only one — "

ALMA. He loves me — he says I'm beautiful — he loves me — *(Beat.)* I love him — *(Beat.)* "I love you too Gene."

PART V

EUGENE. I go to New York once a month to visit. I've been going for a year but I don't care. I know I'm seeing Alma, and we've decided to get married.

ALMA. Gene is patient with me. Patient when we touch. I can't believe how patient he is — how soft he is.

EUGENE. She's beginning to initiate lovemaking — she's buying underwear and perfume.

ALMA. I can't believe how gorgeous I feel.

EUGENE. It's Sunday — a glorious Sunday morning. Filled up on love from Saturday night. Made love all night long Saturday night and still filled up on Sunday. *(To Alma.)* "You were great Alma."

ALMA. "Mister so were you."

EUGENE. "Let's stay here and never move — we can stay here like this for the rest of our lives — "

ALMA. "Yeah and we can call people to deliver food and then go away — "

EUGENE. "Make up terrific lies for someone else to pay our bills — "

ALMA. "I'll only go out to buy more underwear and perfume — "

EUGENE. "Awright now — "

ALMA. "You like that idea?"

EUGENE. "I love that idea. *(Beat.)* Alma I really am thinking about what I want to do with my life and it doesn't have to be Georgia Pacific does it? I can invade this world if I want to."

ALMA. "There is nothing holding you Gene — INVADE this world!"

EUGENE. "You know, Alma, after our honeymoon, I'm going to take time and really figure out what I want to do. I am not going to let anybody tear me down anymore. I can trust myself Alma and I'm not going to let anybody sway me — No more — I AM GOING TO INVADE THIS WORLD."

ALMA. "We're riding Gene — We're FINALLY riding." *(Beat.)*
EUGENE. I get a call from Daddy to come home immediately. *(Robert.)* "Your grandfather Eugene died." *(Eugene.)* I feel my stomach lurch, just lurch. *(Robert.)* "I need you to come down there with me — I REALLY need you — "
ALMA. Thelma and Mr. Gaines pick us up at the airport. Bourbon, cologne, perfume come at us. Thelma jumps on Gene as if she were a little girl. *(Thelma.)* "Oh Momma's baby's back/ momma loves you/ you're all I have in the world/ my daddy's gone and you're all I have in the world." *(Alma.)* Gene spins her around —
EUGENE. I am about to put my Momma — my mother — into the car but Daddy shouts me down. *(Robert.)* "I'll take care of her" *(Eugene.)* and I say "I can take care of her too, man. I can attend to my own mother — "
ALMA. We drive over to Odelia's and she runs out of the house when she sees us pulling up. I get out of the car and she kisses and hugs me. *(Odelia.)* "Lawd, looka dis! — how good ya does look!" *(Alma.)* The yard — is filthy. There is a stench that is overwhelming and I can't detect where it's coming from. I then look at Odelia. Her body has thickened. Her hair is half straightened and half-nappy. She's wearing pink lipstick and some of her teeth are missing which makes her look like a jack-o'-lantern. This garish looking person standing before me with this jack-o'-lantern smile is my mother and then I realize the stench is coming from her —
EUGENE. When I get home, Daddy signals to me. We sit at opposite ends of the bar. He pours me a drink and pours one for himself. He takes a long pull off of his. A long, deep pull. Frowns. Swallows. *(Robert.)* "Your grandfather left everything to you." *(Eugene.)* I take a drink. "What did you say?" *(Robert.)* "You heard me right." *(Eugene.)* I pour another. "Why did he do that?" Daddy looks at me/ then past me/ way past me. *(Robert.)* "I work hard all my life/ I SWEAT all my life and you get everything handed to you — just HANDED to you. Nobody and I mean nobody ever gave me anything — NOBODY — and you wanna know why? 'Cause I was too black and ugly that's why and you wanna know the first person that told me that? My father. He said that to me for as long as I can remember. *(Robert's father.)* 'Boy why you so black — why you born ta me?' or 'Why you can't be like da res' o'

41

da niggas. You go off doing all dat book learnin like da white man — jes' sit yo' black ass down!' *(Robert.)* I was somethin like you Eugene but then I saw what the world was — IS. I saw. *(Beat.)* The world doesn't like black black boys at all. I learned through salt/ sweat and splinters in my ass. *(Pauses.)* Why do YOU get to have it so easy? Why YOU? Look at your hands — my God they're soft like a girl's. You got to have strong hands in this world Eugene. Strong hands, but then again, maybe you don't have to 'cause as soon as people see you comin — high yella people like you, the world stops and moves around you." *(Eugene.)* Daddy leans against the bar says in one of the strongest Geechie accents I've ever heard, *(Robert.)* "You a big time yella nigga now, huh?"

ALMA. I go into Odelia's house and see more of the same. Clothing thrown all over the place, dishes piled high, empty food cans, gin bottles and more gin bottles. I change clothes and begin to clean the house. Odelia looks at me smiling. *(Odelia.)* "seem like old times you being home and cleaning. Wit Eugene Sr. dyin dat mean you an Gene REALLY gon be livin good."

EUGENE. The next day me and Alma go over to grandfather Eugene's house — MY house. It feels strange saying that. My house. The house is huge — there are four bedrooms. I walk through it sneaking sips off my flask 'cause you can't tell me any minute he ain't going to come down the stairs. I stop in the hall by the stairs and it hits me — my head filled with bourbon, it doesn't matter — it hits me. I can see that he had to fight/ he had to fight to get this house — this palatial looking house — he had to fight to prove he wasn't a "light-skinned punk" — he had to fight/ he had to be hard. I understand now why the house was left to me. *(Beat.)* We bury Grandaddy. No great funeral. We just bury him. We have the wake at Momma and Daddy's house. Relatives from Momma's side whom I never met, never dealt with, come up to me, kissing me. *(Voices.)* "Oh isn't it so sad?/ You have to keep the family going." *(Eugene.)* They barely speak to Daddy. They know Alma and I engaged. They smile at her and shake her hand. They do not kiss her.

ALMA. I'm looking at all these fair, thin-lipped people. They look me up and down, past me/ even through me. Mr. Gaines comes over to me reeking of bourbon, *(Robert.)* "Look at 'em Alma —

look at all these yella red niggas — Doesn't it make you sick?"

EUGENE. Momma's happy that her family is present. She's kissing all these people she hasn't seen in years — Some blonde woman comes over and kisses me. *(Voice.)* "We got to stick together — the family is getting smaller."

ALMA. No one is talking to me —

EUGENE. Who are these people? I need a drink.

ALMA. Wyce comes in. He nods in my direction. I turn my head —

EUGENE. *(To Wyce.)* "Wyce, Man, I am so glad to see you man! How the hell did you get leave?" *(Wyce.)* "I got my ways — sorry about your loss." *(Eugene.)* "Thanks, man." *(Wyce.)* "Damn Gene, you got a nice looking family!"

ALMA. Wyce is in seventh heaven with all these people in the room. He's walking around with a bourbon bottle filling glasses. He keeps filling Eugene's glass — Mr. Gaines looks at me, winks, smiles, and fills his glass again —

EUGENE. Wyce is trying to talk to one of my cousins. He keeps telling her, *(Wyce.)* "I had no idea Gene had such beautiful women in his family."

ALMA. How can these people drink in this heat? All of these people are just drinking and drinking — it's like one big buzz.

EUGENE. Mother comes over to me slurring and staggering. *(Thelma.)* "Easy Street boy — never — struggled — a day — in your — life — boy. *(Beat.)* Daddy never respected me or any women for that matter. 'Slap a woman down to keep her in line if you have to.' He wanted to marry me off quickly. He set me up with a boy — a light-skinned boy and the boy beat me. The boy left me black and blue and you know what YOUR father did? He cried. He took one look at me and said crying: 'How could somebody do this to you — you're so PRECIOUS.' Robert is one of the gentlest human beings there is. I can still see him crying. *(Beat.)* My Father didn't give a damn that I was beaten. 'What in the hell did you do to make the boy beat you Thelma — he comes from a good family.' That's what my father said to me. I said, 'Daddy, Robert Gaines stood up for me — he loves me. He takes care of me better than you ever did.' And you know what your grandfather Eugene did? He slapped me. 'You get a little upset 'cause you get a little ass

43

whipping? A man is supposed to keep his woman in line. You marry him — you marry that spook nigger and I cut you off.' So I get nothing and your father got mistreated because he was a gentleman — because he IS a gentleman. You get it all. Why? Why? You get it because you look like him/ you get it all because he wants to get back at me/ even in death he wants to get back at me/ you never had to make any sacrifices/ it's an easy street for you. YOU STOLE FROM ME." *(Eugene.)* I'm getting angry — I feel myself getting hot — angry. Daddy grins and says, *(Robert.)* "Yeah — not only did I lose out — your mother did too — you never thought about that — how YOU took from her." *(Eugene. To Robert.)* "I DIDN'T TAKE FROM ANYBODY! — WHAT THE HELL ARE YOU TALKING ABOUT!"

ALMA. I've never seen Gene like this — I have never seen him drunk like this — I've never seen him violent.

EUGENE. Wyce says, *(Wyce.)* "Take it easy man! Your Mom's just upset — she's had a little too much to drink."

ALMA. People are beginning to leave. *(To Eugene.)* "You've had enough."

EUGENE. "Don't nag me — I can't deal with that right now."

ALMA. "Mr. Gaines, maybe you should tell Gene to take it easy." Mr. Gaines says *(Robert.)* "That's nice the way you're looking after him, God help you — you're taking a lot on." *(Alma.)* He squeezes my backside.

EUGENE. My father squeezes my fiancee's ass. Wyce sees it too. *(Wyce.)* "Man, what did I tell you?" *(Eugene.)* "Tell me what?" *(Wyce.)* "About how the way darker cats see us as punks. I'm always telling you." *(Eugene.)* "Yeah but that's my father, man!" *(Wyce.)* "Yeah even more reason to get at you. Man, if that was MY GIRL?" *(Beat.)*

ALMA. It's dark and everyone is gone except for Wyce. Thelma is very drunk and is crying — she falls off the stool/ gets up/ falls off the stool. Wyce is laughing. *(Wyce.)* "She ain't feeling no pain."

EUGENE. I pour a drink and go outside — it's hot but I need another drink — I need to drink — I don't want to think/ I don't want to see —

ALMA. Robert puts her to bed. He comes out of the house and into the yard staggering — he is now staggering. Wyce follows him and laughs — Wyce is nursing his one drink but keeps filling Gene's and Mr. Gaines' glasses. I tell him, "Listen why don't you stop — you see they"ve had enough!"

EUGENE. I'm drinking and thinking about my father's hand on Alma's ass — groping MY WOMAN'S ASS —

ALMA. Gene's slurring and repeating himself. He's drooling and staggering —

EUGENE. Daddy says, *(Robert.)* "You pretty high/ yella red niggas ain't nuthin — y'all ain't nuthin!" *(Eugene.)* I say "Don't disrespect me in front of my woman — "

ALMA. What is all this "my woman' stuff? He never talks this way — I can't stand him drunk — I HATE HIM DRUNK. I call a taxi and go to Odelia's.

EUGENE. "Man, you've never accepted me. You always giving me shit about being light. I want you to accept me Daddy — I want you to see me for the man I am." *(Robert.)* "You two pretty yella niggas don't know nuthin — easystreet niggas ain struggled fa nuthin." *(Eugene.)* Wyce laughs — he keeps laughing. I can't laugh. "You think it's easy for me don't you? Having ANOTHER NIGGER get in my face 'cause I'm light?" *(Robert.)* "Oh you a nigga now." *(Eugene.)* "No, I'm not — WE're NOT. YOU AND I ARE BLACK MEN — WE ARE NOT NIGGERS." Daddy looks at me and laughs. Wyce laughs too. *(Wyce.)* "I told you, didn't I tell you about how they see us — your father is no different." *(Beat. Eugene.)* Wyce fills our glasses. *(Wyce.)* "Gentlemen, bourbon is truth serum — let's keep it flowing — the truth? Let's keep that bitch flowing — She's an enticing bitch — TRUTH." *(Pause. Eugene.)* Daddy picks up his glass and throws down a shot. *(Robert.)* "I'm a go check on your mother."

(Eugene.) He staggers towards the house and as soon as he gets inside, I break down crying. Wyce puts his arm around me, *(Wyce.)* "Man, I told you? Didn't I tell you — didn't I tell you that he was jealous? He made you feel guilty 'cause you're light. He wishes he were light — IT'S KILLING HIM — HIS BEING DARK — HE HATES HIS DARK SKIN AND BECAUSE OF IT HATES YOU — AND ON TOP OF THAT, HE TOUCHES ALMA THAT WAY? MAN WHAT ARE YOU GOING TO DO?" *(Pause. Eugene.)* His words rip through me/ I break a glass.

(Wyce.) "Hey man, I understand how you feel. He's your father. I understand wanting your father's love but why would your father touch your girl like that? Why would a father want to humiliate his own son?" *(Eugene.)* I look at him — bourbon racing in my head. I look down at my hands. The bourbon has gone from my head to my fists. How'd that happen? How did my fists get balled? *(Wyce.)* "Look, man I gotta go but remember what I'm saying. Father or no father — don't let anybody play you for a punk." *(Eugene.)* I watch him leave.

Daddy comes out of the house, *(Robert.)* "Where's that other pretty red bastard?" *(Eugene.)* "Stop all this 'high yellow this' and 'red that.' And something else man, don't ever put your hands on Alma like that again." He looks at me grinning. He pours a shot and downs it. His eyes on mine. I pour a shot and down it looking back in his eyes. My eyes are glued to his — for the first time my eyes are glued to his eyes. *(Robert.)* "What do you mean?" *(Eugene.)* His voice is so gentle, so smooth — like velvet. "I saw you touch Alma and I didn't like it — don't do it again." *(Robert.)* "You got a house an a lil land and a woman now and you think you can talk all kind of ways to me, boy?" *(Eugene.)* All of a sudden, he's speaking in a Geechie accent. *(Robert.)* "Man dat gal rules the roost — Alma is ga be the one rulin dat roost." *(Eugene.)* "Do you really think so SIR?" *(Pause.)* I feel the bourbon rushing through me. I'm hot/ I'm cold — my eyes never leaving his. He looks at me and smiles. He looks at me — like he's coming/ like his dick is hard — like he's COMING. *(Robert.)* "Nigga jes 'cause I made ya, don mean I love ya — I don love ya and yeah, Ah had touch dat ass 'cause you ain't no man — yeah Ah ha' touch dat ass an Ah'ma touch it again." *(Eugene.)* Bourbon — truth serum is coursing through our veins. I stand looking at his face and he stands up looking into mine. We are now the same height facing each other. My light face/ his dark face. We smell the bourbon on/ in each other. He goes to turn around and I grab him. I draw my right hand back and punch him in the jaw — there is some blood on my right hand. He runs, throwing me to the ground. *(Robert. Yelling/ laughing.)* "Ole high yella nigga ga fight me — Come ON." *(Eugene.)* He's sitting on top on me. I feel his dick on my belly. He's pounding the left side of my face. I push him off, roll over and pick up a chair. *(Screaming.)* "PITCH-BLACK/ APE NIGGA — ANIMAL NIGGA!" He knocks me down and grabs the chair raising it above his head — I trip him. He falls. I get on top of him punching him in the face. *(Screaming.)* "ANIMAL/ GEECHIE NIGGA — BLACK/ APE NIGGA/ ANIMAL." My hands are in his hair — his nappy, nappy hair. I got my fingers in his skull. I beat his head against the pavement. One of my hands goes around his neck and the other hand hits his head against the pavement. He tries many times to get up — he can't. I'm surprised how strong he is — how incredibly strong he is. I pummel him. He continues to yell *(Robert.)* "HIGH YELLA NIGGA! — I NEVA LOVED YOU." *(Eugene.)* I bang his head harder — my groin on his chest — my dick in his chest. Momma runs out and jumps on top of me. She hits me and scratches my face. I keep pounding his head on the pavement until he no longer moves. There is blood on my shirt, face and hands. Some of that blood is mine. *(Lights come up and we see that Eugene is sitting in a private cell.)*

ALMA. I look back — I always look back because now it's so clear. I look back and see me and the rest of us girls. Some of us light, bright damn near white, as they used to say. Others of us darker, brown, black — all of us walking to various rhythms. I remember a girl I met in college at a club for black women. I looked into the eyes of this girl. Her gray eyes. My brown eyes. I looked into her eyes and said, "What are YOU doing here? This club is for BLACK women." She exploded/ cried/ told me she was as black as I was. I destroyed her rhythm/ I burned down her walk. *(Beat.)* I think of the darker girls — girls like my roommate who wore their darkness with pride and how she my roommate and other girls dark like her painted their full mouths the colors of light and dark fruit. They painted their full mouths lushly, sensuously — color rippling from their full mouths. I laughed at the dark girls who wore bright colors and hated the light girls no matter how nice. I am my mother's daughter after all. I had no walk/ voice of my own. *(Beat.)* Two months after the night of the murder Eugene was sentenced to twenty-five years to life. *(Pause.)* Two months after the night of the murder, I knew Eugene's baby was in me. I just knew. I went to Odelia's. She was passed out from gin. I closed her bedroom door and I pushed furniture back and forth.

I just started pushing furniture back and forth. I felt a pain in my groin — almost overwhelming. Later that night in the bathtub, I saw the fetus — the fetus came out in the bath. I could not risk having a child — ugly like me — I could not risk being left to dog-pant. I sometimes dream of the fetus. I dream of Gene holding this fetus he knew nothing about. I dream of this dead baby *(Catches herself.)* — fetus — in a bathtub and Gene holding it. I dream of him holding this dead fetus in his cell. *(Beat.)* I live in New York. My feet hit the pavement. As I hit the pavement, I no longer hear any great rhythm /I was a child/ it was twenty years ago/ everyone's feet hit the pavement. I do not care about summer or fall. It is merely an adjustment/ a change of clothing. I am Odelia's daughter. Listen to my voice/ watch me walk.

EUGENE. I think of soft Southern women like Momma and Alma. That's the thing that is — was — so great about Alma. She's in New York now — that's the last I heard — but I remember her softness. When I think about that summer before she left to New York I think about a dress — a summer dress that floated when she walked in St. Stephen — that dress gave her an incredible softness — a softness that only girls from the South have. When she got to New York, there was that quick/ slick/ glide but in Carolina she simply floated in this dress. I always think about that dress. It was a lilac dress that kinda fell off the shoulder. And there was a day she wore the dress and was wearing a lilac perfume — a soft-smelling lilac perfume. She was wearing the lilac perfume and wearing her lilac dress. I said, "Alma you look soo good in that dress/ you really do/ you look good/ why'd you have to look so good?"

End of Play